FRACKING DAKOTA

FRACKING DAKOTA

Poems for a Wounded Land

By Peter Neil Carroll

First Edition

Published by Turning Point Books
P.O. Box 541106
Cincinnati, OH 45254-1106
www.turningpointbooks.com

Manufactured in the USA.

Cover photograph: *Natural gas flare, White Earth River Valley,* Sarah Christianson, ©2014

Designed by Debra Turner

Library of Congress Cataloging-in-Publication Data
Peter Neil Carroll

Fracking Dakota Poems for a Wounded Land
ISBN: 9781625491220
LCCN: 2015930497

For my children

Matt & Jo

Natasha & Adam

ACKNOWLEDGMENTS

About Place Journal:	"Progress"
American Atheneum:	"Not Going Home"
Cultural Weekly:	"Seeing Something"; "Wake"; "The Woman Next Door"
HEArt Journal Online:	"Aliens": http://heartjournalonline.com/current-issue; reprinted in *Verse Daily* web-weekly feature, http://www.verse-daily.org/webweekly.shtml
Heavy Bear:	"Sleeping with Bears": http://www.heavybear.janecrown.com/HB2/HeavyBear.2/
Lummox:	"Finding Red Bird"
Pacific Review:	"Billboard Bible School"
Sand Hill Review:	"God's Controversy with California"; "Lombardy Spring"; "Footing "; "Keepsake"; "Redwood Valley Road"; "Dusk"; "California Arrival"; "The Catch"; "Land's End"; "Passages"
Southern Humanities Review:	"Dawn"
Turtle Island Quarterly:	"Fracking Dakota" http://fourdirectionpoetry.wix.com/turtleisland#!issue2-chapter3/c1dny; reprinted by Borderbend Arts Collective http://www.borderbend.org/8/post/2013/12/fracking-dakota.html
Work Literary Magazine:	"Workers in Paradise (Alabama)" http://www.workliterarymagazine.com/submission/peter-neil-carroll-11252013/

Thanks

I offer special thanks to my Saturday Morning poets—Casey FitzSimons, Esther Kamkar, Muriel Karr, Harry Lafnear, and Lee Rossi—whose affection and honesty have created an intense but supportive environment. Charlotte Muse and Richard Silberg also shared their opinions of the evolving manuscript. I give thanks to my hosts at various readings for the opportunity to test my voice aloud: Joyce Jenkins of Poetry Flash; Christine & Dennis Richardson of Willow Glen; Ramon & Judy Sender of the Odd Monday Series; Sandra Anfang of the Rivertown poets; Sherri Rose-Walker of the Know-Knew and Florey's series as well as the usual suspects at Coastside, Not Yet Dead Poets, and Waverley Writers. Also, much praise for this book's appearance to Debra Turner of dtDesign. And thanks to Sarah Christianson [sarahchristianson.com] for permission to use the cover photo. My pal Michael Batinski shows up in these poems in more ways than I can say, an astute observer and sounding board. Jeannette Ferrary remains my favorite poet and creative inspiration.

Contents

PART 3
KEEPING THE MOMENT JUST BEFORE

PART 4
WHO WILL LOSE FOOTING FIRST

PART 1

MAPS,
DREAMED IN THEIR HEADS

Fracking Dakota

The skinny woman behind the bar pops
bottle caps with both hands, never stops.
She's lived five years on Bakkan Basin, a sink
of oil, natural gas. *Big changes*, she brags.

Clear skies in summer, tawny hills swoop
to the horizon, spacious
as a dry ocean, maze of yellow-browns
hinting at tangles underground.

High-pressure chemicals pour
through earthen cracks, promising oil,
four billion barrels, enough to make
normal people tolerate turmoil.

A farmer in overalls crosses the blacktop.
I don't see another human for 160 miles
except a driver at the crest of a 24-carat acre
taking pictures of sunflowers.

The billboard reads: A SMILE INCREASES
                    YOUR FACE VALUE

Humans live off camera, leave traces:
fence wire, water tanks. Coils of hay
ripen by the roadside. A shed implodes,
silver tags hang from the cows' ears.

A white pickup scorches over yellow lines
to pass five eighteen-wheelers, racing
head-on into traffic. The driver veers
left into the dirt, gray spirals rising,
shoots back two lanes, a man in a rush.

At Ludlow, a craftsman carved a cross high
as an A-framed church; in Buffalo, a thresher
hovers like sculpture. Over Bowman
a crop duster crawls, the pilot a shadow on glass.

Taxes gettin' high, complains a man
on a barstool. *Yeah,* says the guy working
his sixth Fat Tire beer, *now I got to buy*
flood insurance. Paying the tab, thumbs
pick open a roll of hundred dollar bills.

At the center of a flaxen field splashes
of unearthly blue break the spectrum,
oil pumps bowing toward the land
like mechanical horses drawing oats.

The woman brewing coffee says blue pumps
aren't worse than silver windmills. *Those men,*
her head tips vaguely west, *send paychecks*
home; an' when the boom's done
the digging stays underground, I hope.

Tanks shaped like hayricks cast
shadows on fresh-mowed wheat. Swarms
of spidery backhoes grind into
the soil. A gas-flare tints sooty air.

The underworld carries dreams of power.
Fractured earth belches, coughs up gas,
vapors lured from darkness. The bedrock
prepares to heave, wakening its demons.

Birds of Dakota

Old Highway 2 leads to a steel fence
far off the road. Circular tracks wait
for the mobile multi-warhead vehicles.

Otherwise only hay fields, cows, a silo,
red barn, hills reaching to the sky—
a distant train of tankers freights east.

The Bomb sleeps underground, its
brain, organs, vessels hard-wired.
A gray terminal guards the software.

The officer looks twice, head
to toe, decides to tell me the story
of a farmer pestered by blackbirds:

*You see, he fired three shots
into a peach tree, a flock of helicopters
landed, soldiers asked him questions.*

I start over. At the airbase, a tour bus
passes the runway of antique bombers—
B-29, -36, -52.

Glossy white, Minute Man 2 sits
80-feet deep in concrete. Its warhead
arms in ten seconds; 1.2 megatons.

Inside war is woven: cable, batteries,
sextants; ghosts of warriors, physicists,
engineers; the air cold, time frozen.

Launched once, the rocket test-coded
to a vacant field, its fire too fast
for human eyes. The wheat sizzles.

The Wake

The walleye flat on shell-rock sand
attracts a buzz of blue-bottle flies.
The fish I ate roils my stomach.
Here lies its cousin baking in sun.
Two more come bobbing into shore,
pushed by the wake of a speedboat
spitting blue exhaust. The current cares
as little as the sailor, as the sand
on the beach. The lake smells
fishy. The walleyes swallowed
more toxin than I did. Only flies feast.

Flag Day

Stars & Stripes droop from iron lamps,
the gazebo's painted in bunting. Old soldiers
guzzle links of grilled Bratwurst and beer.
Red-faced, tattoos faded, they laugh
like boys who glued gray whiskers, got fat.

Falling behind, I parade brick-paved streets
past an oak-shaded park, groups clustering
near the pond. *For the Beauty of the Earth,*
says the white-washed Congregational Church,
we raise our hymn of grateful praise.

I hang around for the action—
firecrackers, brass band, the mayor's greeting.
Folks in rayon chatter
about this and that, distracted
by a buzzing microphone.

Mosquitoes attack. A mother slaps
sunscreen on her boy's back,
oils his shoulders, asks *Where's Daddy?*
and seeing him, waves to the man holding
a yellow balloon in both hands.

He kneels by the lake, sets his trophy to sail.
My eyes fix as the wind lifts it
like a feather over water and around the bend.
Gone, he calls. Still I wait—
and turning, see the boy also waits.

Harvesting the Blue Fields

South down one side, north up the other:
as the postman I carried mail in a pouch,
now leaflets on a clipboard, doing my bit
to bring out the vote.

I knock, deliver the pitch, wait for a smile,
a nod—or apoplexy. Everyone's nice
sometimes. *You have got to be crazy, yodels*
the soprano: *Him? Never.*

A black man rocking on his porch rouses
the Doberman, *sic, sic.* Fright shoots off
my skin. But when the citizen grasps
my purpose, he kicks the dog, slaps my palm.

The day a 20-mile hike, front doors loom
like the Great Wall. OXYGEN. NO SMOKING.
A woman near tears saying *Health care, please,*
squeezes my hand, keeps me moving.

My chimes at a red-brick house bring a lady
wearing a pearl necklace, her best smile, soon
growling I'm not her property man, shocked
at the candidate I support.

What issues? *Jobs,* she says, adding
Not my family. Her head tilts closer,
lips tight, confides
We don't need black in the White House.

Faith swerving, I keep knocking, consider it
good news when no one's home. One man kills
the throttle on his mower, shouts, *I'm 70.*
I don't give a damn. And I'm glad I asked.

Sweet Lorain

The beach alive with a thousand
gulls, pale waves thrash Erie's shore.
I trudge the dunes, scattering
flocks to kneel before sweet water.

I cup clarity to my lips. Half a mile
inland, downtown Lorain weeps
like a lover awakening to find
the other side of the bed empty.

Everywhere is FOR LEASE. The grand
Citizens Savings Association, letters
cut into stone, replaced by yellow
plastic, FIFTH THIRD BANK.

The Legion features Chicken Karaoke. A
cosmetology school vies with WIGLAND.
Bargains galore! The workers club sells
four shots with beer chasers for ten bucks.

Inside the campaign office, everyone's
from somewhere else—Rico, Sara, Patrick;
Boston, LA, Jersey—confident
as Jacobins, history will turn, now, here.

They say the future's in the streets
where no one ever is. Five days I sing
to sweet Lorain, has she changed her mind?
Maybe it will rain, they'll stay inside.

Not Going Home

I don't want to tell you, the woman confides.
Not my business, but nice she's polite,
hasn't slammed the screen so far.

Stranger in a brown leather coat, I go
door-to-door, writing replies. Their eyes
narrow. I hear obfuscation, fear, lies.

I look twice before answering
a bald man who rolls down his window,
announces he's finally back in town.

Sometimes you can't go home.
I don't want to go home, he swears.
It's still the same. That's why I moved away.

Half hour later, his horn beeps, interrupting
my jay-walk. All smiles, my new friend
discovers someone who'll listen.

People think the damnedest things.
He shakes his head, befuddled.
They heard I was dead. Can you imagine?

Strangers

I'm in trouble,
searching my seams
for quarters
as lawyers beeline
through shadows
to Ford Explorers.

Time's expired,
no one in the booth
giving change.
The hurried woman
hugs a leather brief case,
shield against the night.

Twice I cough,
show the $1 bill.
All fluster, she dips
into her bag,
rummages,
hands me 75 cents,
won't touch my money.

Gosh, everyone needs help
some time.
And God bless you.
Please.

I force the dollar
into her fist.
To make you
an honest woman.

Alone after sundown,
best not to get
personal. What if
she screams?

Billboard Bible School

Why Question God When We Know He's Right?

Through school bus windows
dutiful daughters read
signs of the future life.

Heaven is sweet,
Hell is not.
You are going to one,
Ready or not.

Until their own
expectant bodies show
the signs.

CHILDREN ARE A GIFT FROM GOD

Their dutiful mothers—
also daughters—
let public signs speak
their silence.

Abortion Is Never The Answer—CHOOSE LIFE

And the fathers
who never were
nor will be daughters
insist
abstinence makes the heart
grow fonder.

This Year Thousands of Men Will Die of Stubbornness

Amen

Milton, West Virginia

Uncle Dave's been dead
four days. He's so happy,
the preacher marveled.
The whole time
he hasn't given us a thought.

Ozark Evangelical

He is Risen!
He is Risen!

Hairdresser 1 (Suspicious): Do you go to church?
The Customer (Hesitant): No, I'm a Jew.
Hairdresser 1: (Calling) *She is!*
Hairdresser 2: (Calling back) *Poor thing!*

To Be Almost Saved
Is To Be Totally Lost

I Hadn't Held a Rose

so close, tickled
by dense perfume.

Her children moved
in turn, one
carried the urn.

Beneath a piñon tree, one
spilled white ash
on desert earth.

One stripped the rose
scattering red on white.
One planted a vertical stem.

She gave us the world, one said.

I placed a round red stone
to shield
her slender pile.

Clouds gathered.
We left her where thistles
wouldn't harm the view.

Morning at Spiro Mounds

At the crest of holy ground,
cloud-piercing light quickens
the wings of blue butterflies.

A thousand years ago, a woman
cracked walnuts with rock, shucking
husks into buckets to make dye.

Her jewelry—bone earrings, necklace,
finger rings—grave robbers have taken.
Her name is long lost.

Here a masked shaman sighted equinox,
eclipse. I picture her eyes brightening
at the miracle of caterpillars.

Natchez Trace

Maps, dreamed in their heads,
they memorized shadows, ghosts
lingering between trees.

Road signs for distance
guide the traveler
through thickets of time.

A plaque marks missionary work,
fields cleared by slaves. Miles later,
a Chickasaw village raided, burned.

Paths of power run straight: land *ceded.*
Passive voice, language without blame.
Mash barrels swapped for chattel.
No romance on the trail—buyer beware.

The Return of Billy the Kid

The most dangerous street in America
if you believe Rutherford B. Hayes—
William the "Kid" Bonney blazed
his six-shooter at a posse
galloping through Lincoln, New Mexico.

I'm almost there when a black pickup
swerves into a cutout, heaving dust,
misses my front bumper by an inch.
Sun vertical, I find shade inside
an adobe diner with a short menu.

Through old glass, I watch the black truck
pull up. A lanky cowboy clatters in.
"How you doin', Bill?" calls the cook.
Mean as ever. Been talkin' all morning.
Some sheep down the road....

Admiring a wall of frontier relics—
milk-glass door knobs, granite spatula,
bottles, spools and spikes—
I hear him ordering chili beef,
potato salad, coffee, the desperado
bragging, *I got a big appetite today.*

How's your goats? the cook wants to know.
The cowboy pinches thumb and forefinger.
You know who owns tomorrow?
A little guy. You don't own a thing.

He wolfs the meal, stands up gleaming,
slips a toothpick between his lips.
Clearing out, he yips, boots going bang-bang.
The engine roars, a cloud rises.

He's heading east, looking toward the odds
he can't beat, the Mescalero Apache casino,
its one-word billboard tempting the lost—
      FORGIVE.

PART 2

LETTING
THE DOGS SLEEP AT NIGHT

Grant's Tomb

Scholars add 100,000 names
to the Civil War dead
but counting changes
no battle's end.

Truth wavers. Stories survive.
Every listener a teller claiming
wisdom. Hearsay, anecdote, repeat.
A remembering voice starts over.

No witness left to reply, the rigid
live on, sepia-stained
in grotesque positions, each one
a fact, artifact, sometimes a lie.

The End of Negro History

Down in the Delta, I play
records for the teachers:
Paul Robeson's basso amazes
them. Lady Day's
Strange Fruit brings sorrow.

They say they never heard those voices,
remember from the old days
only the homeboy Richard Wright.
His uncle survived the *incident*
and they talk three hours
like thirsty people, of lynching, shotguns
loaded by the door.

The new syllabus begins
with *Brown* and Mrs. Parks, touches
the teen Emmett Till, too sweet
to know not to whistle at women.
Martin, Malcolm, LBJ thwart
old man filibuster. Much easier
to praise progress, good
defeating evil, let
the dogs sleep at night.

Aliens

It's what you can't see in Alabama,
a kid's soccer ball hidden in the shed,
someone's mama behind a curtain
waiting for sundown to go outside.

I hear the pickers fled the state,
fields red with broken tomatoes.
No cook to fry a taco—the white man
boarded up Rico's Cantina.

After the preacher went, leaving
the *Iglesias* locked, thieves
stole a silver chalice, baffling police.
All the usual suspects had vanished.

One matinee features a civil rights
movie. When it goes dark at the end,
no one, white or not, leaves their seats.
No one wants to face the light.

Under Cedar and Oak

The nuclear plant hides
behind mist in gray outline,
steel gates unattended.
Red signs invite visitors
to leave *immediately*.

Spooked by movies
of mutant ants, I make
a fast turn, drive
past abandoned houses
rotting in rain. Panic
doesn't stop until I reach
a circle of markers
topsy-turvy under cedar and oak.

Weather has eclipsed the names:
Colonel Finley. Some letters—E z h—
crusted by dirt and dead leaves.
My finger scrapes. Bones buried
before the Civil War, plantation
masters used granite, marked
their servants with raw boards.

In minutes, a poison leaf, subtle
as uranium, inflames my hand.
I persist. She is somebody.
Eventually, mistress or slave,
Elizabeth, I free her name.

Workers in Paradise (Alabama)

CARTHAGE

No place to eat in rural towns
I pick apples at Piggly Wiggly,
distracted by loud shouts:
a cock-eyed, toothless man
disputes the register printout.
Where's my buttermilk! My shrimp!
Two checkout women
laugh hysterically.
One covers her mouth, whispers
I love Tuesday, he does this every Tuesday.

COURTLAND

Not a shop seems open on Main
but three rusty pickups squat
outside a shuttered door. I push
inside. An elderly chef, her flowery dress
touching the floor, calls out

God bless! and dishes sweet potatoes
baked with pecans, collards,
ham hocks, beans, and gravy. Her partner
in Church of God T-shirt delivers dessert:
I sure hope this beats pie in the sky.

FLORENCE

My lodge of choice might have at least
one working light bulb, one thin towel,
a plastic cup.

The harried manager, a newcomer
with wife and kids cramped rent-free
in a franchised dump, scrambles
to please a paying customer.
Poor man, we meet in every city,
over his head in cracks and grunge,
busy, busy, striving.

Selma

Two black gents stretch on lawn chairs
surrounded by heaps of watermelons.
I might laugh or weep at stereotype
but this city's reputation
can't be ruined, not Selma.
Where folks forced a President
to say on prime time

We shall overcome—and they have,
mostly. Downtown could use a speck
of polish after they take down
          CONDEMNED
signs and fill the vacant rooms.

Three drug stores thrive on Main.
Half dozen churches, a synagogue, give
salve for the soul. Leaving town, I wave
to the sleepy entrepreneurs, waiting
patiently long past the cusp of history.

Ancestors

Voluptuously green,
oak and pine circle
the ghost village, dwellings
of an ancient people
near a slow river.

Artisans beat copper
into bracelets, carved pipes
shaped like serpents, decorated
with human hands, eye
of a bird trapped in the palm.

Drought sent them away,
or war, their ways lost
but not different
from settlers who came
to fish, sow corn,
import their own slaves.

Progress

You know where you stand in Mississippi
goddam.

Outside the capitol, white marble honors
Our Mothers, Daughters, Wives, Sisters,
ladies of a Confederacy.

Senator James Eastland Courthouse salutes
an ornament of bigotry and injustice.

On a dark street, a neon bus flashes
pink, marks the spot,
mobs attacking Freedom Rides.

They name the reservoir shimmering
in early sun for Governor Barnett, lover
of segregation, who let billy clubs rain.

There's peace in the streets.

School bells invite students inside,
black ones know to follow.

Trail of Tears

My finger follows the map, curving
from a village in Georgia
to the southern tip of Illinois. In winter,
where glaciers scooped a gorge,
the uprooted cover their dead.

A bugle hurls the path southwest, sped
by missionaries for God's progress.
Sequoya translates the Bible
into Cherokee; he too is conveyed
to Oklahoma, pushed by faith.

Ribs stab through emaciated skin.
On sacred mounds once tall as pyramids
the wind shakes yellow willows. Not
the cry of barefoot women. Not
the children's whine: the witness weeps.

Finding Red Bird

He flinches when I say the name,
though he's never gone in.
Be careful. It's all black.
Don't ask for directions.

Off the main road a turnoff
breaks through brush, gravel kicking
columns of red dust. Behind jungles
of weed, houses tip, roofs sink.

A rusty, bullet-scarred marker
doesn't exactly mean
      WELCOME TO RED BIRD.

Freshly lettered street signs cross
South Main. East Hartford.
No road bisects the spot.
He'd warned me
Be out of town by sundown.

White-washed, the Baptist church
is shuttered. Nearby I glimpse
yellow, purple flowers, first sign
of life, wreathes upon a grave.

The sun broils, dust polishes
my shoes. I follow tombstones:
The Walkers living to 90,
buried 1946. In sandstone:
Gert May Harris died 1916.
S B Bradley, Asleep in Jesus.

I come up behind a man limping
on a cane, shapeless fedora shading
jet skin. I don't ask for directions.

The Tourist in Me

I'll tell you about visiting my fiftieth state
from Cimarron hills to the streets of Muskogee.
Oklahoma's a great place to get lost.

I'll show you Eufala Lake and a hotel in Poiteau
promising NO RAILROAD NOISE! not far
from the last stop on the Trail of Tears.

I'll bring my stories: twelve attempts to find
Oklahoma's all-black towns.

How I forgot to visit the art museum in Tulsa,
but found a good plate of catfish, red beans,
okra at Smoke House Bob's. And about the day

I met a stringy-haired mechanic in Wagoner
grinning as he sketched directions to Tullahassee.
There I met a black woman with an arm
of bracelets, lost on her way to Wagoner.
The waitress winked, sold us each a map.

Oklahomans agree on basics: high speed limits,
no billboards about abortion, cancer, or gambling.

Most folks struggle. Their skin sheds into grass
day by day, sweat replenishing dry fields
with flowers whose names I forget.

Remind me to tell you everything else I missed.

Mixing

The motel keeper, Hindu
by name, skin, dress, speaks
without shame
on a cell phone about
her husband's infidelity.

A dark-complexioned waiter laughs—
No hay cerveza, amigo—
reminds me the county is dry.

Two Seminole women claim
the "all-black" historic town
is neither black nor white
nor red all over.

No white person can steer me
to a hamlet called Taft,
but I see a husky black man staring
at an engine block look up
with surprise, saying
You're here. Turn right.

Liquid voices, country drawls,
the pitch of laughter echoes
Oklahoma songs—
this land is yours, Will Rogers,
Woody Guthrie. I hear
mothers whispering to babies.

Second Chances

Rexall Drugs becomes a flea market,
marble soda fountain sparkling
with second-hand watches.

Jewel Theater goes dark, reopens
as a dance hall, sells nipple rings
to the man who has everything.

Fred's Furniture & Appliances calls
GET IT TODAY! WE WONT BE BEAT!
and just as a couple chooses the love seat,
CLOSED. NOW LEASING! NOW RENT TO OWN!

City fathers replace
fluorescent street lights with faux
Victorian lamps, luring the quaint.

A law firm occupying Smith Hardware offers
          Divorce without Drama
home repairs to fix the broken hearth.

The faithful falter. Storefront churches shutter-up,
assuring the remnants
               FAITH MAKES THINGS
               POSSIBLE NOT EASY
hints of the Second Coming, Rapture.

Never say die, the hucksters grin.
A missionary's work is never done.

PART 3

KEEPING THE MOMENT
JUST BEFORE

God's Controversy with California

Drought, the preacher chides,
God's punishment for a sinful people
besotted with superfluous waters—
sipping pinot noir on the Sabbath,
baptizing pretty babes in hot tubs.

But today the blue skies darken, drains
thump like lovers' hearts, the excited
lemon tree promises more fruit.

Tomorrow I'll plant pomegranate seeds
under the clouds, tempt them to stay.

Time now for a steamy bath, soup
for dinner, willow wood in the fire.

Chosen people, how quickly
the universe forgives.

Keepsake

A woman carves
big letters in beach sand
THIS IS CRAZY
watching the sea stealing
her confessions of love.

I lift a black stone laced
with white agate, slip it
into my throwing hand,
count the number of skips
it would make
if I gave it to the waves.

On my desk it will keep safely
along with my chunk of the Berlin wall
and a bronze chit
from the Silver Dollar Hotel,
GOOD FOR ONE SCREW
Madam Ruth Jacobs, Proprietor.

One good screw may not last long
but crazy, lost at sea, is forever.

The Wishing Tree

Under an olive tree in Port Costa
near Suisun Bay, a hundred paper leaves
tied by white strings, dangle from frail branches,
their messages faded by weather and wind.

I wish for more vacation.

I wish peace & love for all my loved ones.

I wish I would have been kinder and more loving
to my dying mother.

I wish for rain and snow.

I wish for a happy and healthy baby, due May 1.

I wish everybody loved me.

Just someone who understands
the dark corners of my mind.

I wish for a magical life filled
with awe and gratitude.

I wish that the truth will come to light
and heal the confused.

I wish to lose 50 lbs of my weight in 2 years.

I wish I was with Jessica.

COURAGE

I wish I would go to a great college. Ashley.

I wish to feel full & free.

I wish to meet the love of my life.

I wish the person who reads this
will know how much they are loved.

I wish my friend could cure his depression.

I wish I was an Oscar Meyer Weiner.

I wish my luck would win me
limitless trips to Disneyland.

I wish for my brother's safe return from China
and a dog.

I wish the Raiders go to the Superbowl.

I wish you enough love.

I wish to travel & see many things.

I wish to always remember
the peacefulness of this tree of wishes
and feeling the breeze on my skin.

Pelican

Her beak picks a salty itch, one wing
hectic, the other poised. Into her brown
stare, I whistle one tone three times
then repeat. She will not echo.

I purse my lips, kiss into the wind.
Her silence disapproves, I think.

I leave her perched on a wooden rail
just above the woman staring
at the sea who will not hear
my laughter or scratch what itches me.

Lombardy Spring

Happiness, pleasure, love, these sentiments
rate low, on what Americans think
they should pay for, says my Hungarian friend
Tibor, expert on the value of money.

He advises me to spend my dollars
buying gardenias, tulips, daisies, roses—
flowers bringing perfume indoors,
signifying love, pleasure, happiness.

But that was his complaint:
You people (his accent Hungarian) *don't consume
enough flowers and keep them forever
to dry like a long marriage.*

Water was his secret ingredient.
He took me to Lombardy Spring
in the coastal range, filling plastic bottles
with soft water to fortify his blossoms.

He laughed when I told him
I prefer water from the tap.
I picture Tibor, brows raised,
admiring my stupidity.

He's gone now, his ashes
covered by violets and lilies;
and Lombardy Spring lies under a ton
of rock beneath the widened highway.

When I find faded petals in a book,
I remember Tibor's crooked smile
and wonder if a fool like me
bought too many or waited too long.

Interstice

Headlights redden
the doe's eyes.
She leaps
before I brake,

takes me back
to the filmmaker shooting
a battle and his own murder,
his footage dizzying to black

and to the photograph
of a rabbit staring at a gun flash
the instant
a bullet pierces its flesh.

Animal surprise freezes
the eye, holds the image
forever, meaning never,
never knowing.

Not clinging, not letting go
I try to love that way,
keeping the moment
just before.

Seeing Something

I start with the eyes, see something
of myself that sparkles when I make a quip;
the crease of her mouth, the teeth, the gap,

how her thin upper lip covers the healthy bite
she reveals only later when she really cracks up,
and I discover the color of her lips is the same

as the tips of her breasts. But what keeps my eye
is the surgical scar, two-inch keloid near the nipple
that insists laughter won't last forever.

I touch the healed rim furtively, unready
to admit the skin's fear is my own; each dimple,
nick, blemish, the body's mark against eternity

summoning. I cling, press into her folds, pull
to the wound like a man diving off the dock,
geysers of seawater tossed toward heaven.

Afloat on the bed, seeing something of myself,
I say, *You're a lucky woman.* She, seeing something
of herself, hangs on, saying, *And you're a lucky frog.*

Just Us

We're in bed again
entranced by shapes
in the knotty pine ceiling.

Above my pillow, a one-eared rabbit.
Above hers, Saturn and its rings.
A shooting star would flare
if we open the curtains.

We never do.
Over our feet, a big crack
like the equator. We avoid
the tropic zone, keep

out the glare that flays our solitude.
However the day begins,
we end like this, one after
the other, knowing well

what will follow. Soon.
She asks the age-old/
old-age question:

Shall we switch sides?
I grumble.
Now I've gone too far.
She climbs across, I slide under.

(Does she think,
when the reaper comes,
the one nearest the door
goes out first?)

We contemplate Saturn's circles,
raccoon eyes staring
back, warning:
Sooner than you think.

Lost in Sleep

The person on the other side of my bed
doesn't sleep. Her eyes close,
body motionless, I watch
her nose squiggle, catching a scent.

In the morning she tells me dreams, how
she searched dark corners for lost objects:
keys, a contact lens,
the carefully drawn map, a blind man's dog
that mysteriously vanished.

Blindness, keys, maps—such
secret desires to have and not hold.
What she keeps becomes her captivity.

In her nightmares, she meets the man
who lives on the other side of her bed.
She's never surprised to find him.

I won't be coming home, he announces.
I waken to find the bed empty.
She's gone out to search for something
she can't live without.

Running Water

*Scientists have found the sound
of running water compels beavers
to build dams.*

—Museum Plaque,
Bosque State Park, New Mexico

HARD-WIRED

The aseptic urological surgeon confesses
while scrubbing in his greenest scrubs
he feels nine times out of ten a sudden urge
to urinate, concludes his mother sixty years
before opened faucets to teach him when.

HEARING THE FALLS

Pine-rimmed springs splash
down stony rills while silent men
in yellow helmets glance
at passing joggers glancing back.

Flood destroyed the bridge. Runners
unaware, shuffle feet impatiently.

Two species: One eager. One stalls
to stretch the overtime.

WASHING DISHES

She rubs a yellow cloth inside ceramic cups,
soaps the dishes, spoons and forks, runs
the tap until my birthday platter sparkles
on the board. It's time. Her neck,
her breasts, my hands against her hips.
How I love the sound of running water.

She Turns

Under eucalyptus, a red Toyota gleams
on the bluff. She's locked the doors.

Two wide-winged pelicans wheel
above the sun-lathered shore.

The woman turns from the sea, pictures
two children, two cats. Him.

Back she turns—low waves washing
stone, beating, beating, two steps—

and like a waterfall spilling
into the seductive swell,

a woman plunging into her bed—
shoes, arms, hair—she leaps.

Drowning

An undertow lurks offshore
slurps the round rocks—
    clok, clok.

It isn't not knowing that leads me.
My friend stays back, timid
as I am bold. Through thin soles,
I feel the rocks rolling—
clok, clok—dance lightly,
reach water's edge unharmed.

At a good foothold, I anchor
on graveled sand, waves addressing
the rock—*clok, clok*—a line of crests
slipping into shore sucks back
and a surge bends the sea upward.

I see it rise by inches, flooding the gap
in which I'm trapped, fills
my shoes, drenches socks,
ankles, knees, my crotch—
pulls me under the sea.

Wallet, dollars, license,
hard proof, my visceral ID
lies wet against my thigh. I may drown,
that thought comes last. I see it
unfold—lack panic, not awe.

The body in reflex, hard-wired,
simplifies reconciliation,
earth to sea. I stretch. I float. Only
dumb weight resists. I see it all,
my tumbling fall.

I hear the ocean's breath. I'm seaweed
bagged upon a craggy point. My pockets leak
like faucets, each shoe weighs ten pounds.
Alone, wet to the bone, no one saw me drown.

PART 4

WHO WILL LOSE FOOTING FIRST

Dawn

It comes like a banner. First light
cracks past the blinds, raindrops
from a midnight shower release
their grip, vaporize, disguise.

It takes a while to learn
warm air rising draws in
the clouds that wait
above the sea. A gray shadow
reveals the front of deception.
Darkness approaches,
rain battering glass
before the coffee's brewed.

To read the newspaper, I turn off the lights—
for what's the point? A front-page photo shows
a Chinese ambassador shaking hands
with the secretary of state; below the fold
archeologists unearth a skeleton
near a village in Kenya.

Electric sky, rain pattering in metal gutters,
I tap to the ragged music. Not for long.

By noon, everything changes again, even
the ambassador's smile, even old bones
exposed to air. The sun is out.

I visit the mailbox, looking for a letter
that never comes, and return with a grocery flyer
offering five pounds of potatoes for a dollar,
red strawberries that will never ripen.

The weather's my excuse. Spring nudges
open the doors, but I stay in the kitchen. I can stay
all day. My mother was like that.
It's what frightens me.

The Woman Next Door

We speak the same language, my trees
and me. More fluently
than I talk to the woman next door.
Scrub oak, cherry plum, lemons, dwarf
pine, olives, willow, redwood—whatever
seeds the birds drop I adopt.

Now she's added a porch
that gives her height, a perch
to watch from. So I walk in my backyard half-
naked, watering pots of cactus, rosemary, dill.
We know each other, living close
for forty years and smile
when our cars pass on the hill.

In summer, windows open, I hear
a shared taste in the tunes we play.
We're lazy, not pruning ivy that overgrows.
But she keeps a cruel eye on my redwood.
Its brother and sister stood tall on her side
before she turned the grove
into firewood. More sunlight, she crows.

Next she'll be saying, more clothes.

Redwood Valley Road

A dozen black-faced sheep, nimble
as ballerinas, slip into the road, nostrils alive.

At the shore, whitecaps pound
continental bone, drill
a perfect arch through a forty-foot shelf.

Above the violent sea
whips of wind press the animate to earth.

A wide-winged hawk breaks
flight, drifts
backward in invisible currents.

Cypress trees tilt like ladies bent on canes.

I follow the ancient trail,
seabed to beach, sandstone to soil.

Seafarers thrilled to cut
the planet's highest spars, redwoods old
as the Roman empire.

Bare cliffs bristle in wind.

At the tree line
loggers quit, green succeeds,
the sign offers 800 ACRES.

A couple stares at the thundering shore.
The ocean decides how long it lasts.

Night Flight

Bulb-bright, street lamps
illuminate the airborne night,
dark fields sliced
by ragged creeks, winding roads.

Neon haze depletes
the shadow's power, dissolves
a human's fear, seeing
eyes flash above teeth.

Then a big moon douses the valley,
rouses a country of insomniacs,
cougar, skunk, raccoon coming
to stalk their property line.

An owl scores the mouse.
The plane creases lunar white,
I lower the shade, allow
my wolves to howl.

Footing

The blue house shudders on a brown hill,
leaves falling from live oak, layer
with pine needles, dry weeds.

I like the hush of mulch, patter
of nocturnal skunks guiding kittens
along ancient trails.

The first time I saw my house,
I found a redwood stump thick
as centuries waiting to be wedged.

Two years I sawed, good exercise for
a desk-bound man; by third Christmas
I held a fifty-pound hunk, almost old as Jesus.

The fire smoldered twenty-four hours.
Its blue odor still tears my eyes,
the loss labors in my heart.

Under living redwood, I scatter
oyster shells from Tomales Bay, pretend
to fill fissures in San Andreas fault.

Whatever boils below, I don't wonder
who'll lose their footing first—me
or the skunks, the house, the brown hill.

Worry

Two inches to the left of my heart,
where the skin is taut but soft,
I've detected a thorny question,
sandpapery,
and my fingers begin
to worry this flag
from an unknown country.

It's what worry is about:
this need to define clear borders,
delineate the healthy native,
face the part that doesn't belong:
of principle, a betrayal;
of choice, the one I'd not prefer,
the one I think I'd never do.

I say I'll do anything
to excise that worry,
scratch, bite, tear,
irradiate my very meat.

I'll do anything
except abandon that alien outpost,
my impermissible self.

Sleeping with Bears

Black bear splinters the front door,
sweat freezes on my neck—
a wild nightmare wakens me—

then I remember
the story, poor Papa Bear,
his house invaded.

Heart pounding, I get
a grip on the darkness,
vow to fix the latch.

For now, wide awake, I count
sheep, tossing, lose track,
finally abandon the covers.

I go out to call on Papa Bear,
have a heart-to-heart
about the bad dreams we share.

Restless under the stars,
he's counting his children. A glint
from *Ursa Minor* lights him up.

Half the year bored in caves,
he stares at the fireworks:
shooting stars, artillery, mortar.

Count your children, he advises,
as a faraway father scrambles
from bed to save his kids.

The old man claws through rubble.
Papa Bear can't quench his excitement.
Bombs away. Better their children.

Yes, I count my children lucky,
feed them porridge, sleep them safely
under quilts, shingles, stars & stripes.

But it's harder than counting sheep:
Someone's broken in again,
eaten up the beds.

Arrival

The western horizon sweeps into a crescent,
luminous as the pale moon.

I take notes with my tongue, the Pacific enlarges my nostrils.
The wind speaks Tagalog.

I cross a strip of sand, dip my hand into gray foam.
Salt drizzles from palm to whiskery chin.

A running dog bumps me into the undertow.
I arise shaking my fur. Kelp clings to my hips.

I am no longer terrestrial. I dwell
with the walrus, the black seal.

This has never happened before; it happens every day.

Dusk

At the edge, waves swarm
against black gravel, swirling
the turbid tide. My feet beg
to retreat. I hold them firm, obey
the rule: NEVER TURN
      YOUR BACK
      ON THE WAVES

Truth is, I savor the crush
of elements—water bounding earth,
air—and my fire within, once
blazed but banked, appropriate
to meet the clouded sky.

Gulls disappear downwind.
Beyond breakers, mysterious foam slobbers
in the stream—dunks and rises,
impervious to mortal time.

Through thick air, I can report
no news of islands. No ships.
Nothing alive but me. A hard gust
heaves my warmth to the sea.

Lit by Stars

The night sea speaks
in half-sighs,
ebbs with a sob. I dispel
darkness by counting

the roll of white crests
coming ashore. Never more
than four. I'm the only
living being to see, hear

no other sound. Black rock
between us, ocean and me.
Until dawn a pair
then one gull cries, twice.

Nothing Clear

At land's edge, nothing clear but
the shock, high seas bashing rock.
The continent looms and ends.

High seas dizzy me, tilting
horizons, swamping shores.
Even firm places give ground.

I enter the blur of elements, seams
threaded between bodies, uncertainty
of where I stop and you begin.

The Catch

Twenty-foot waves thunder
against sprawled rock, remnants
of broken cliff. The men fishing
keep their eyes
on gray-green crests, wild
as animals. A pelican leaps
into the wind. Pigeons pick
slivers of bait. Eyes turn to a trapped crab
measuring too small, watch the man
throw it back. The wind quivers
glass poles, boys clumsy
with tangled lines. *No fighting,* Emilio calls
to the sea, banter covering bad luck.
The men know the ocean's violence, how little
a day's work matters to the world,
how much one fish will mean.

Snowy Plover Beach

Beyond wiry grass curled
like fur, wind-brushed, banked
by dunes, a man in a red wool cap
sips from a thermos. Beyond him,
a long-beaked plover speed-walks
at the lip of sudsy surf, pausing
every ten steps to peck a morsel
bubbling in sand.

Beyond all, the ocean throbs, pulling
my body, its pulse patterned
after the waves, a pair
of pendulums falling into twinned
rhythm, continuous, universal.
Ribbons of lace wind around my feet.
I pierce the cadence to soak my fate.

Geese

A wedge, geese honk up the coast,
and two long-necked stragglers
pass quietly a minute later, flying
in formation. One leads,
the wing pilot just behind.

They couple efficiently, though
they've lost the flock. As I have,
one by one. Most mornings
I drink tea with a single friend. Not long
ago noisy chairs surrounded us.

Land's End

Climbing the high ridge, sun
pinching eyes, I feel the sea's intimacy
recede. The leashed dog lunges, sets
a pace. My breath tightens, chill wind
on my face.

Avoid altitude
the doctors warned. I slacken
only slightly, breathing harder, can't help
but wonder why I take the risk.

Up here where hills stretch, rumbling
waves vibrate to the pinnacle. Far below
a surfer paddles over a crest, falls
backward, still paddling, as I struggle
ahead, intoxicated by what
I imagine may be last thoughts.

Against Extinction

A boy skipping on tarmac races
ahead of brothers, father, grandfather—
all older, but the bones don't change,
two gap-teeth bare ancestral proof.

We pause in antiquity, visiting
luckless creatures who sank
in asphalt pits, lay for centuries
under wind-blown sand. The kids howl
into the jaws of saber-toothed cats.

Acrobatic dragonflies still skim
over simmering tar to mate mid-air.
Among a million fossils, one human
sleeps—a woman trapped with a dog
10,000 years. Only she touches light.

Like animals that drowned, I devour
wild salmon, dance my tail in circles,
wail to the wild moon. A child asleep
in her mother's shawl keeps
the genes alive a little longer.

The Sun Falls

Finally the sun falls, blushing
a wispy sky. Along the beach,
hand-holding couples amble
toward niches.

I wander the other way, searching
abandoned wharves, drawn to
a fog horn, slivered moon,
waves fingering land's edge.

For a moment, I intrude on earth's
intimacy—rock, sea, wind, darkness
descending—watch the tide
consummate insatiable desire.

Passages

"...this frigate earth is ballasted with bones..."
—Herman Melville, 1851

When I played
under the kitchen table,
I didn't know
old people slept
in rooms below.

I ran over grass in a city park,
high clouds made me dizzy. I lost
my footing, overheard trees
giggling. I could not face them.

When I lived in the middle
of the country where lakes
glowed blue and the Mississippi River
slid like a torrent
through my heart, the most sensual
color was earth-dark chocolate.

Gray now, I hear
Pacific whitecaps grinding rock
into sand. I'm cargo
on a gallant ship,
tooth, bone, tissue
sailing the growling sea.

About the Author

In *Fracking Dakota*, Peter Neil Carroll, poet and historian, travels the natural landscape looking for America's human soul. His previous collection of poetry, *A Child Turns Back to Wave: Poetry of Lost Places* (2012), won the Prize Americana from the Institute for the Study of American Popular Culture. An earlier volume, *Riverborne: A Mississippi Requiem* (2008), explores the lonely world of America's great river. His poems have appeared in many journals, including *About Place Journal, Cultural Weekly, Heart Journal, Lummox, Pacific Review, Review Americana, Sand Hill Review, Southern Humanities Review, Turtle Island Quarterly, Verse Daily,* and *Written Rivers.* He has published over twenty books, including the memoir, *Keeping Time* (2011). He has taught creative writing at the University of San Francisco, taught history and American Studies at Stanford and Berkeley, hosted "Booktalk" on Pacifica Radio, and edited the *San Francisco Review of Books.* He lives in northern California with the writer/photographer Jeannette Ferrary.